The World of Mythology: Norse Mythology

By Jim Ollhoff

VISIT US AT
WWW.ABDOPUBLISHING.COM

Published by ABDO Publishing Company, 8000 West 78th Street, Suite 310, Edina, MN 55439.

Printed in the United States of America, North Mankato, Minnesota.
112010
012011

 PRINTED ON RECYCLED PAPER

Editor: John Hamilton
Graphic Design: Sue Hamilton
Cover Design: Neil Klinepier
Cover Photo: Gonzalo Ordóñez
Interior Photos and Illustrations: Alamy-pgs 12, 14, 15, 17, 23, 27, 28 & 29; AP-pg 11; Christoffer Wilhelm Eckersberg-pg 22; Emil Doepler-pgs 16 & 26; Getty Images-pg 7; Granger Collection-pgs 19, 24 & 25; iStockphoto-border icon; Mårten Eskil Winge-pg 21; Mary Evans Picture Library-pg 8; Photo Researchers-pg 9; RobRoy Menzies-pg 13; Thinkstock-pgs 4, 5, 6 & 31.

Library of Congress Cataloging-in-Publication Data

Ollhoff, Jim, 1959-
Norse / Jim Ollhoff.
p. cm. -- (The world of mythology)
ISBN 978-1-61714-726-5
1. Mythology, Norse--Juvenile literature. I. Title.
BL860.O66 2011
398.20948--dc22

2010032590

Contents

THE MIGHTY MYTH

Myths are stories that are important to people. Some myths tell people how the world works. Other myths teach people how to act with one another. And other myths tell people how to find meaning when life becomes difficult.

All people need stories. We need stories that give us a beginning, a journey, and an end. We can see ourselves in the characters of the stories. When we read about a goddess who was heartbroken, we say, "I've been heartbroken before, too!" When we read about a god who did a noble deed, we say, "I want to be like him!" People such as the Vikings told stories about courageous gods to help their warriors be more courageous.

Myths are stories that help us make sense of the world. Myths give us meaning. They make life more understandable. Even today, when we watch movies and read books, larger-than-life characters make us want to be like them—or not like them. We need myths as much today as the Norse people did more than 1,000 years ago.

Left: A carving of a Viking warrior.

Above: Norse people told stories of gods who were courageous and smart in battle.

The Vikings

Thousands of years ago, tribes of people settled in the lands of Norway, Sweden, and Denmark. They hunted, fished, grew grains, and raised cows and sheep. These people came to be known as Norsemen, or "men from the North."

In 793, one group of Norsemen sailed across the North Sea and attacked and robbed an English monastery at Lindisfarne. This was the beginning of the Viking Age, which would last for more than 200 years. In the Old Norse language, the word *víkingr* (Viking) referred to a warrior or sailor who went on raiding or settling expeditions overseas. In Old English, the word *wicing* (Viking) simply referred to someone who was a pirate. For centuries, English monks uttered this prayer: "From the fury of the Norsemen, O Lord, deliver us."

Viking ships on the sea.

Most Vikings lived in today's Norway, Sweden, Denmark, Greenland, and Iceland. They expanded their influence eastward to Russia, and south to the Mediterranean Sea. In about 1000 AD, they even made a temporary settlement in North America, at a place called L'Anse aux Meadows. The small collection of buildings was located on the island of Newfoundland, in northeastern Canada. It may have been used as a base for further exploration of the new continent.

Left: A man wearing traditional Viking clothing.

While most Vikings were traders, fishermen, and farmers, the Vikings were most famous as furious fighters. They ransacked villages across Europe for 200 years. Shortly after 1000 AD, the Viking influence declined. More centralized foreign governments and better coastal defenses made Viking raids less profitable. The influence of Christianity also played a part in taking the fight out of the Vikings, as well as replacing traditional Norse mythology.

A Sturdy People

From the fiery lava flows of Icelandic volcanoes to the frozen tundra of the Arctic Circle, Scandinavia has always had a harsh climate. It takes sturdy people to live there. Scandinavians' severe existence is also reflected in their mythology. The Norse gods were harsh, warlike, and fierce.

Contrary to many of the mythologies of the world, the Norse gods were not intimately involved with humans. The gods were in a different world than humans, and they rarely had contact with mortals. They lived mainly with the other gods, and also giants, elves, dwarfs, and other magical beings.

The stories we have about Norse mythology were written down in long poems called *sagas*. They were told by word of mouth for hundreds of years, and finally written down starting around 1200 AD.

A society's mythology always tells us something about its culture. The gods and goddesses of Norse mythology were a sturdy bunch, just as Scandinavian people had to be. The gods and goddesses performed feats of great bravery, just as the Vikings were required to do. In the place where the gods lived, there was a great hall called Valhalla, where the spirits of heroic human warriors who died in battle went to be honored. The Vikings told these stories to help their warriors be courageous and brave.

The Scandinavian people, like their gods, were sturdy and fierce.

Norse mythology remains with us almost every day. Several of the days of the week are named after Norse deities. Tuesday is Tiw's day. Tiw, or Tyr, was the Norse god of justice. Wednesday is Woden's day. Woden is the Germanic name for Odin, the king of the Viking gods. Thursday is Thor's day. Thor, the god of thunder, was a much-loved god of the Vikings. Friday is named after Frigg, the queen of the gods and wife to Odin.

Monday	Mőnandæg	"Day of the Moon"
Tuesday	Tiwesdæg	"Tyr's Day"
	Tyr was the Norse god of justice.	
Wednesday	Wődnesdæg	"Woden's Day"
	Woden/Odin was king of the Viking gods.	
Thursday	Pűnresdæg	"Thor's Day"
	Punor/Thor was the god of thunder.	
Friday	Frigedæg	"Frige's Day"
	Frigg was the queen of the gods.	
Saturday	Saturn	"Saturn's Day"
	Saturn was the Roman god of the sun.	
Sunday	Sunnandæg	"Day of the Sun"

Above: Several of the days of the week are named after Norse deities.

Above: Gollum is one of the characters from J.R.R. Tolkien's *Lord of the Rings* series.

Another place that Norse mythology continues today is in the popular *Lord of the Rings* movie series. The movies were based on books written by J.R.R. Tolkien. Tolkien borrowed heavily from Norse mythology, including concepts such as enchanted rings, elves, dwarfs, and different "Earths" from our own.

Norse Creation Myths

In the beginning, according to Norse mythology, there were two worlds: the frozen land of Niflheim, and the fiery land of Muspell. As the cold and heat mixed, frost formed. Eventually, the frost became a cruel ice giant named Ymir, from whom more frost giants were created. A giant cow also appeared and fed Ymir with her milk. The cow began to lick giant cliffs of ice to get water. After licking the cliffs for a long time, the cow uncovered a man who was buried in the cliffs of ice. This man was the grandfather of Odin and his two brothers.

When Odin and his brothers grew up, they went to war against the evil giants. They killed Ymir, and formed the Earth with his body and the sky with his head.

As Odin and his brothers were walking near the ocean one day, they saw the logs from an ash tree and an elm tree. From those trees they created the first man and woman, giving them life, intelligence, and beauty.

Above: Norse myth says Odin and his brothers created the first people from trees.

Above: The ice giant Ymir.

Asgard and the Tree of the Universe

The Viking myths talked about a universe with three levels, all connected to a giant tree. Each of the levels had several worlds, such as the world of the elves, or the world of the evil giants. It was possible to get from one world to another, but such travel between worlds was rare.

On the top level was Asgard, the place where the most important gods lived. Another world on the top level was the home of less-important gods, and the world of the light elves. In Asgard, there was a hall called Valhalla. Brave human warriors who died in battle would be taken to Valhalla. Odin's servant Valkyries, female warriors on flying horses, would choose the most courageous warrior souls and take them to Valhalla. There, the human warriors feasted, fought, and prepared for the final, universe-ending battle with the giants.

Odin and brave warriors in the great hall of Valhalla.

Above: Armed Valkyries enter a battle on flying horses.

Left: The Norse god Heimdall guarded Bifrost, the rainbow bridge connecting Asgard with the human world of Midgard.

On the middle level was Midgard, which was where the humans lived. Between Midgard and Asgard was a rainbow bridge made of fire, called Bifrost. This was how dead human warriors made it to Valhalla. But not just anyone could use this bridge. Guarding the bridge was the god Heimdall. He could see for hundreds of miles, even at night. His hearing was so good that he could hear grass grow. With his magic sword, he protected Asgard from anyone trying to enter uninvited.

On the lowest level of the universe was Niflheim, the frozen world of the dead. The ruler of the land of the dead was Hel, the monster daughter of the god Loki.

A giant tree held the universe of worlds together. There were others living in inhabitants of the tree as well. A giant snake lived at the base of the tree, constantly gnawing on the roots. The fates lived in the tree and tended it to keep it alive. An eagle lived at the top of the tree, keeping watch over everything. And a little squirrel named Ratatosk constantly ran up and down the tree, carrying insults between the snake at the tree's bottom and the eagle at the top.

Above: According to Norse mythology, a giant tree held the universe of worlds together.

Odin: The King of Asgard

Odin was the undisputed king of Asgard. He was the god of battle, wisdom, and poetry. He created most of the worlds, and he created people. From his throne, he could see all the worlds in the universe. Two ravens, named Thought and Memory, sat on his shoulders and told him the news of the day. He was sometimes pictured with an eye patch or a hat slumped over half his face, because he only had one eye. He traded the other eye for a drink from the Well of Wisdom. He also had enchanted rings and a spear that never missed its target.

Odin could take the shape of anything, and would sometimes appear as an old man to humans on Earth. He was not a benevolent, faithful father figure. He was fickle, and his allegiances depended on the moment. He would sometimes help a human army win a battle—or cause them to lose a battle—if it suited him.

Left: Odin sometimes appeared with a hat slumped over half his face because he only had one eye.

Above: The Norse god Odin on his throne, holding his spear Gungnir. By Odin's side are his two wolves, Geri and Freki, and his two ravens, Huginn (Thought) and Muninn (Memory).

THE MIGHTY THOR

Perhaps the most beloved god in Asgard was Thor, the god of thunder. He had a bushy red beard and carried a magic hammer. While Odin was more aloof and self-absorbed, Thor was compassionate and good-natured. He was a friend of farmers, and felt like one of the common people. However, he could be ferocious and strong. When thunder and lightning appeared in the sky, people thought they were seeing the effects of Thor fighting the giants.

Thor's weapon was a hammer, which he could throw at his foes. Whatever he aimed at, he struck. And the hammer would always return to him, like a boomerang.

One story tells of a giant who stole Thor's hammer. The giant was getting married, and so Thor dressed up as the bride to sneak into the wedding. He almost gave himself away by eating too much at the wedding meal (he ate a whole ox). When the giant brought out the hammer to show the guests, Thor grabbed it and dispatched the giants.

Thor's hammer was called Mjöllnir. It was often worn as a pendant.

For people of the Viking Age, Thor was the most-worshiped of the gods. Many people used the name "Thor" in their name to honor him. Even today, many place names in Iceland and Norway begin with the syllable "Thor," named in honor of the god of thunder.

Above: Thor, the god of thunder, wields his mighty hammer called Mjöllnir.

The Other Gods of Asgard

There were many other gods who lived in Asgard, although Odin and Thor were the most important. Frigg was Odin's wife, the queen of Asgard, and the goddess of marriage, children, and households. She could see the future, but couldn't do anything to change it. She spent a lot of time weaving the clouds.

Bragi was the god of poetry and beautiful speeches. It is from his name that we get our word "brag." Freyja was the goddess of fertility and agriculture. Her twin brother, Freyr, was also a god of the crops.

Balder was Odin's son, the gentlest of the gods. He was wise and full of grace. Frigg, his mother, foresaw that he was going to die. In a panic, she tried to protect him by getting every living thing, plant and animal, to swear that they wouldn't hurt him. Every plant and animal did, except the mistletoe flower. All the other gods had fun by throwing rocks and trees at Balder, knowing nothing could hurt him. The spiteful god Loki, however, made a dart out of mistletoe and threw it, and Balder died instantly. Frigg's tears became the berries of the mistletoe. Later, Frigg foresaw that Balder would eventually return from the underworld. She was so happy, she hung the mistletoe above her door and promised to kiss anyone who walked beneath it. This holiday tradition continues today.

The death of Balder.

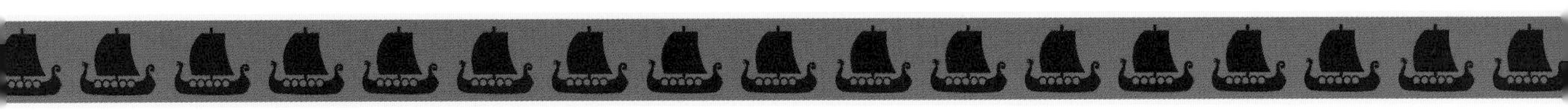

Above: Frigg was Odin's wife, and the queen of Asgard.

Enemies of the Gods

The gods of Asgard had many enemies. Chief among the enemies were the giants. The giants were at constant war with the gods, because it was Odin who killed the giant Ymir at the beginning of the world.

Another enemy of the gods was Loki, who actually was one of the gods himself. He was a complex character, because sometimes he was good. He was cunning and clever, and always knew how to get the gods out of a jam. However, he was spiteful and mean as well. Sometimes he played mean tricks for fun, and other times he was downright destructive. After a while, the gods tired of his mischief, and put him in chains.

One of Loki's children was Fenrir, a huge monstrous wolf. The wolf was so ferocious that the gods realized he must be put in chains. They tried to chain him, but he was so strong that he easily broke his bonds. Finally, Odin and some dwarfs constructed a magic rope that would hold him. Only Tyr, the god of justice, was selfless enough to risk tying Fenrir up with the rope. Fenrir bit off Tyr's hand, but the evil wolf was finally restrained and no longer dangerous.

Right: The Norse god Tyr loses his hand to the bound wolf Fenrir.

Above: Loki, the god of mischief, cuts the hair of the sleeping goddess, Sif, Thor's wife.

SHIELDMAIDENS AND VALKYRIES

Women were important in Norse mythology and folklore. Women called shieldmaidens sometimes fought on the battlefield. Some are mentioned by name in the Norse sagas.

Possibly inspired by the shieldmaidens were the Valkyries. These were female servants of Odin. Different Norse sagas tell different things about the Valkyries, and some of the stories conflict with each other in the details. For example, some sagas say there were only three Valkyries. Others say there were 27.

A Valkyrie carries a hurt warrior.

Above: In some myths, the Valkyries were ferocious, and in other stories, beautiful.

The earliest myths identify the Valkyries as ferocious spirits who enjoyed the bloodshed of battle. In time, however, the Valkyries became beautiful women with long blonde hair who selected the souls of the bravest of the dead human warriors for Valhalla. Sometimes, the Valkyries would rescue heroes from terrible danger. In some stories, Freyja, the goddess of agriculture, is the leader of the Valkyries.

Ragnarok: The End of the World

The Norse myths are unique because they predict exactly what will happen at the end of the world. The stories say a great final war will occur between the gods and the giants. This final battle is called Ragnarok.

When there are three winters without a summer, then the battle of Ragnarok is ready to begin. Loki and the wolf Fenrir will break free of their chains and join forces with the evil giants.

Above: Ragnarok, the final battle between the gods and the giants.

The gods and goddesses of Asgard, along with the warriors of Valhalla, will prepare for battle. Earthquakes will shake the worlds, and mountains will crash to the ground. The sagas even identify which god will fight which giant. Fenrir, the giant wolf, will kill Odin. Odin's son Vidar will then avenge his father's death. Thor will destroy a giant serpent, but not before the serpent sinks deadly venom into Thor. Heimdall, the bridge guardian, will battle Loki, and both will fall in the battle. Fire will engulf all the worlds of the universe.

After the fires go out, the Earth will slowly come back to life. Balder will return from the underworld, just as his mother predicted. Balder, his goddess wife, and a few of the minor gods who survived the battle Ragnarok will sit on the grass where Asgard had once been. Two humans, a man and woman, will also survive Ragnarok and will repopulate the world.

And so, after the terrible devastation of Ragnarok, a new world will emerge. It will become a golden age of peace.

Right: After the final battle of Ragnarok, a world of peace will emerge.

Glossary

Asgard

The world where the gods live.

Bifrost

The rainbow bridge connecting Midgard, the world of humans, with Asgard, the world of the gods.

Midgard

The world of the humans.

Mjöllnir

The magical golden hammer belonging to Thor. Although the handle was a bit too short, it would hit any object that it was thrown at, then return to Thor's hand.

Niflheim

The frozen land of the dead.

Odin

The king of the Norse gods and ruler of Asgard. His name is also spelled "Woden." Wednesday is named after him.

Ragnarok
The final battle at the end of the world.

Ransack
To overrun a place, stealing whatever can be found, and destroying what's left. For 200 years, Vikings were most famous for ransacking villages across Europe.

Sagas
Long poems that tell the myths of the Viking Age.

Shieldmaidens
Women who chose to fight as warriors on the battlefield. They are mentioned in Norse mythology's stories and sagas. Shieldmaidens may have inspired the creation of Valkyries.

Valhalla
A hall in the world of Asgard, holding the souls of the bravest human warriors who died in battle.

Valkyries
Horse-riding female servants of Odin who carried dead warriors to Valhalla.

Venom
A poisonous liquid that some reptiles, such as snakes, use for killing prey.

INDEX

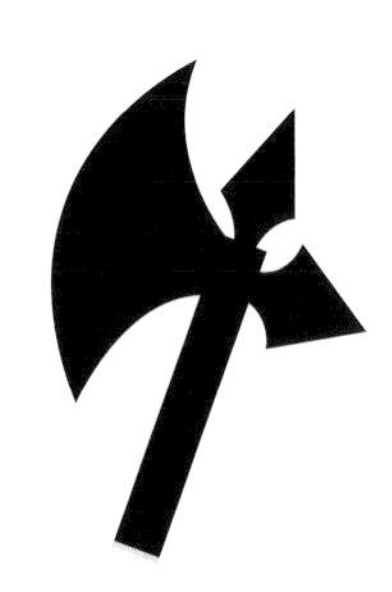